בס״ד
D1030301
לה׳ הארץ ומלואה
This Siddur Belongs To:

My First Sing-Along Siddur by Rabbi Aron Rabin

1st Printing - January '09 / Shevat 5669 • 2nd Printing - October '09 / Tishrei 5770
3rd Printing - February 2012 / Shevat 5772
4th Printing - November 2014 / Kislev 5775

Order online at www.myfirstsiddur.com
email: info@myfirstsiddur.com

CREDITS

Photography: Carlos Chattah - photosbycarlos.com
Layout & Design: Aron Rabin - aronrabin@gmail.com
Set & Script Coordinators: Nechoma Rabin & Shaina Baumgarten
Editor: Sheina Herz **Contributors:** Dovid Weinbaum, Raizel Weinbaum, Leibel Baumgarten, Penina Baumgarten, Rivkie Pink, Rochel Goldberg, Rochie Pink
Music: Chony Milecki - Recorded at Chony Milecki Studios www.SimchaTunes.com
Vocals: Benny Hershkowitz, Eli Marcus
Child Vocalists: Chayale & Avrohom Goldberg
Venue: Home of Yirmi & Chani Knight
Cast: Benny Attias, Danny Attias, Rachel Attias, Yael Attias, Gabriella Chattah, Eliana Cohen, Sara Rivka Duchman, Charlotte Hamburger, Sophie Hamburger, Zoe Hamburger, Yaakov Mendel Handwerger, Kehos Herz, Mendel Kaller, Sara Freida Katan, Yossi Katan, Mendel Katz, Bassie Knight, Berel Knight, Rivka Gittel Levy, Eli Rabin, Shaina Rabin, Tzivi Rabin, Nava Taieb, Ava Turetsky, Chana Zissel Zavilowitz

ISBN: 978-0-615-24393-1

The Aleph Beis

ו Vov	ה Hey	ד Daled	ג Gimmel	ב Veis	בּ Beis	א Alef
ך Final Chof	כ Chof	כּ Kof	י Yud	ט Tes	ח Ches	ז Zayin
ע Ayin	ס Samech	ן Final Nun	נ Nun	ם Final Mem	מ Mem	ל Lamed
ר Reish	ק Kuf	ץ Final Tzadik	צ Tzadik	ף Final Fey	פ Fey	פּ Pey

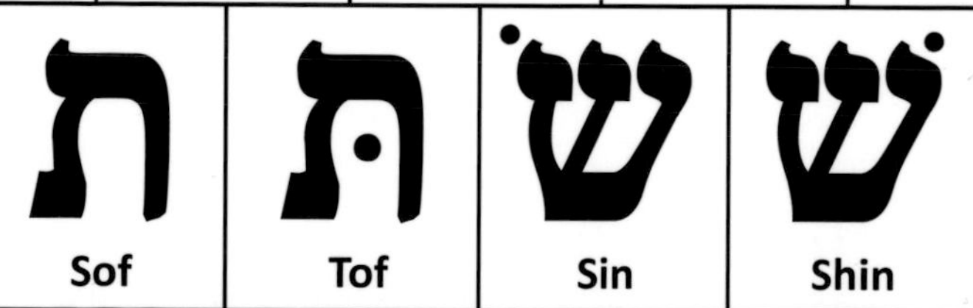

Chataf Segol	Chataf Patach	Chataf Komatz	Shoorook	Koobootz	Cheereek	Cholam	Sh'va	Segol	Tzeirei	Patach	Komatz

The Good Morning Train is coming
How are you? Choo Choo.
The Good Morning Train is coming
How are you? Choo Choo.

The Good Morning Train is coming
The Good Morning Train is coming
The Good Morning Train is coming
How are you? Choo Choo.

And we'll say hello to Eli,
How are you? Choo Choo.

And we'll say hello to Shaina,
How are you? Choo Choo.

And we'll say hello to Tzivi,
And we'll say hello to Mendy,
And we'll say hello to Benny,
How are you? Choo Choo.

978-0452

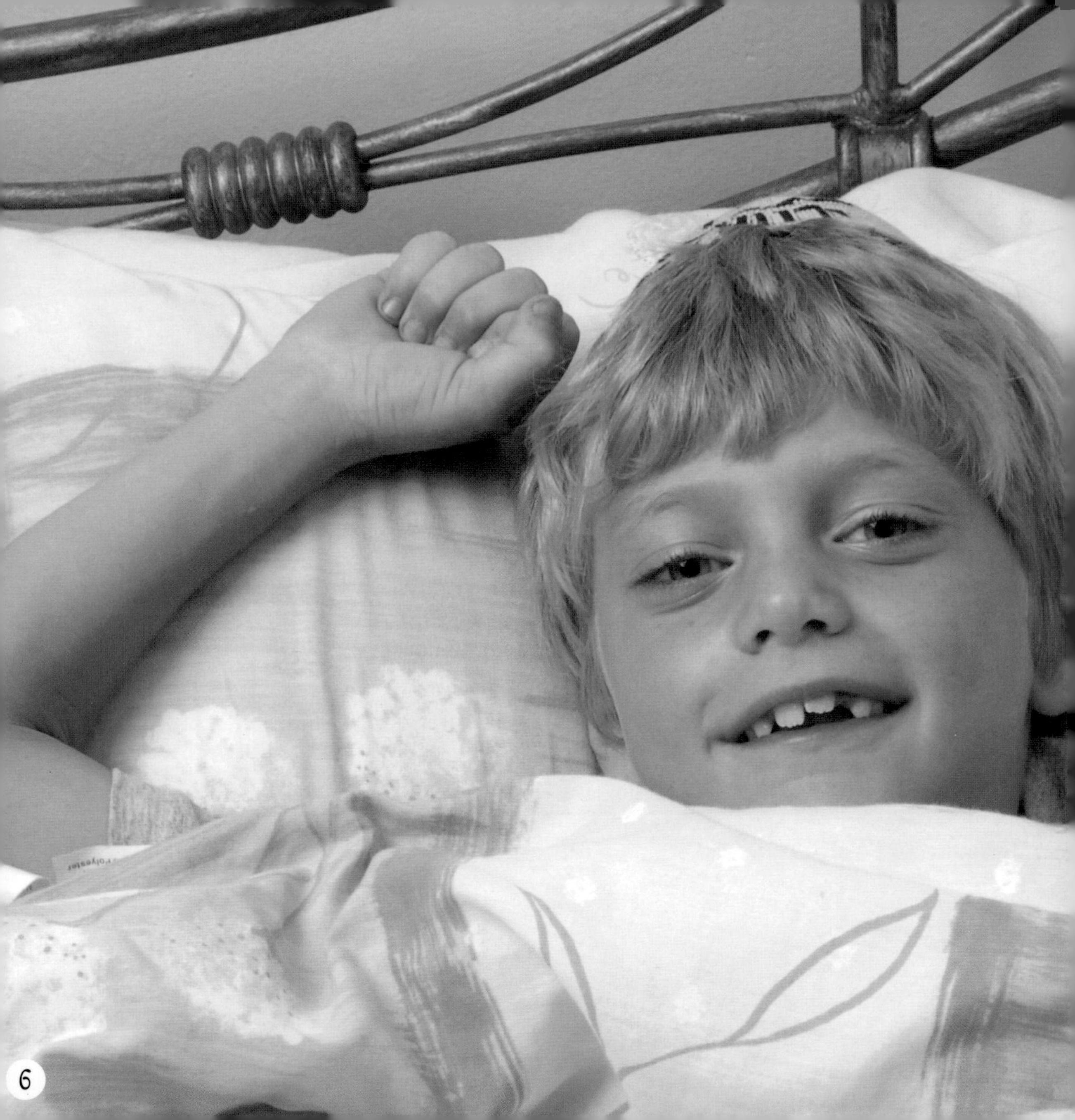

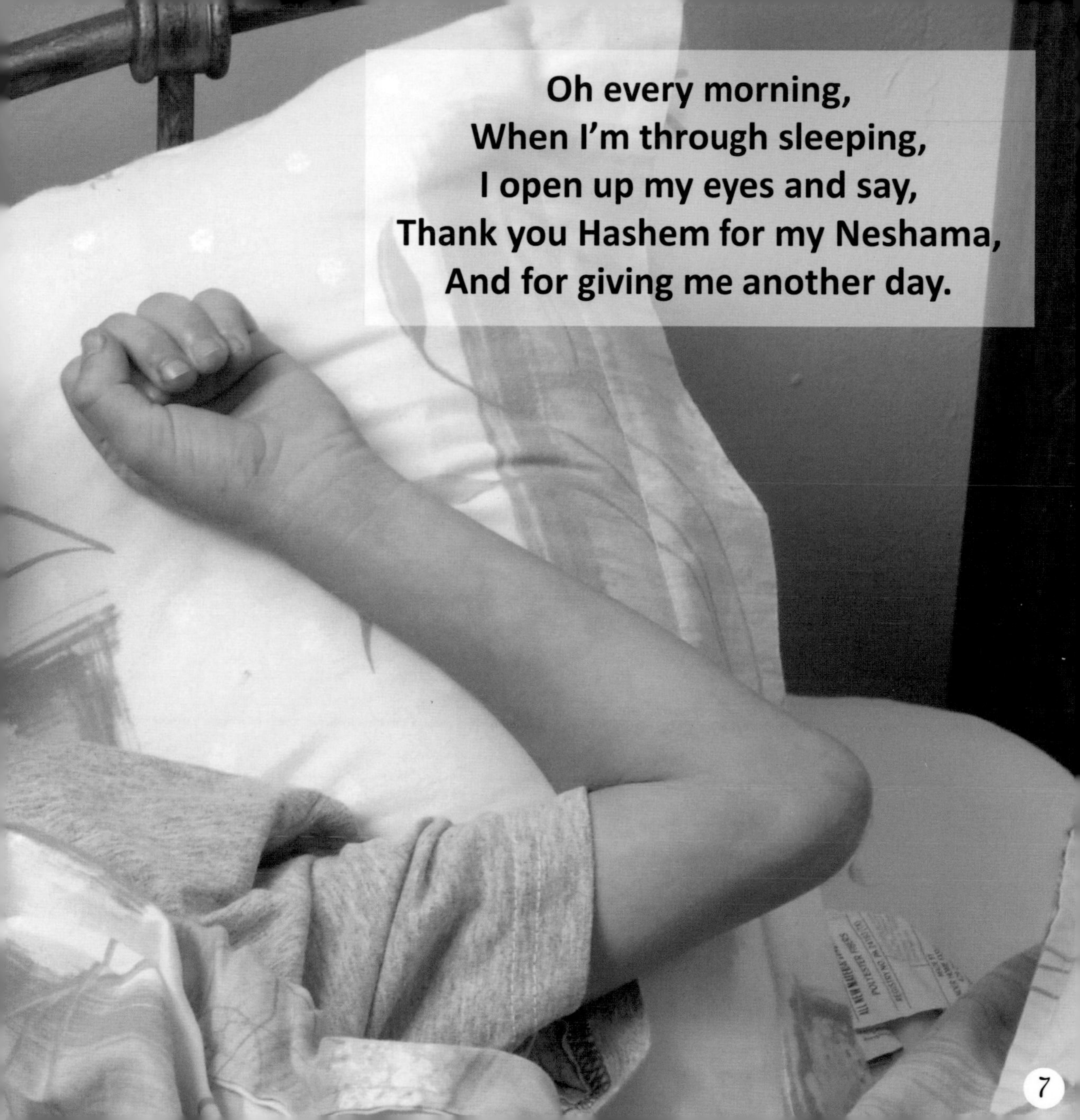

Oh every morning,
When I'm through sleeping,
I open up my eyes and say,
Thank you Hashem for my Neshama,
And for giving me another day.

We open one eye, we open two,
We say Modeh Ani
'Cause it means thank you.

We wash our yadayim,
Six times that's true,
That's what every Jewish boy and girl must do.

THE COW IS IN THE BARN,
IT GOES MOO, MOO, MOO
THE TRAIN IS
ON THE TRACK,
IT GOES
CHOO, CHOO, CHOO

THE BIRD IS IN THE TREE,
IT GOES TWEET, TWEET

ALL ARE SINGING MODEH ANI

מוֹדֶה אֲנִי לְפָנֶיךָ מֶלֶךְ חַי וְקַיָּם,
שֶׁהֶחֱזַרְתָּ בִּי נִשְׁמָתִי בְּחֶמְלָה.
רַבָּה אֱמוּנָתֶךָ.

Modeh ani l'fonecho Melech chai v'kayom,
she-he-chezarto bi nishmosi b'chemlo.
Rabbo emunosecho.

I offer thanks to You, living and eternal King,
because You have mercifully given my soul back to me;
great is Your faithfulness.

This is the way we wash our hands,
Wash our hands, wash our hands,
This is the way we wash our hands,
So early in the morning.

Once on the right and once on the left,
Once on the right and once on the left,
Once on the right and once on the left,
So early in the morning.

בָּרוּךְ אַתָּה יְיָ, אֱלֹהֵינוּ מֶלֶךְ הָעוֹלָם, אֲשֶׁר קִדְּשָׁנוּ בְּמִצְוֹתָיו, וְצִוָּנוּ עַל נְטִילַת יָדָיִם.

Boruch atoh Adonoy, Eloheinu Melech ho-olom, asher kid'shonu b'Mitzvosov, v'tzivonu al netilas yodoyim.

Blessed are You, Lord our G-d, King of the universe, who has sanctified us with His commandments, and commanded us concerning the washing of the hands.

Hashem gave us a present,
Do you know what it was?
He gave us the Torah,
And we must keep its laws.

He asked the other nations,
"Do you want this gift of Mine?"
But they said, "No thank you,
For Torah we've no time."

Then to B'nei Yisroel,
Hashem did go,
We said, "Na-aseh V'nishma,"
Because we love Him so.

Then to B'nei Yisroel,
Hashem did go,
We said, "Na-aseh V'nishma,"
Because we love Him so.

Mitzvos make
me happy,
Mitzvos make
me smile,
Smile all day long.

Morning, noon and
evening and also
in between,
Six hundred and
thirteen.

בָּרוּךְ אַתָּה יְיָ, אֱלֹהֵינוּ מֶלֶךְ הָעוֹלָם, אֲשֶׁר
קִדְּשָׁנוּ בְּמִצְוֹתָיו, וְצִוָּנוּ עַל דִּבְרֵי תוֹרָה.

Boruch atoh Adonoy, Eloheinu Melech ho-olom, asher kid'shonu b'Mitzvosov, v'tzivonu al divrei Soroh.

Blessed are You, Lord our G-d, King of the universe, who has sanctified us with His commandments, and commanded us concerning the words of the Torah.

Little Torah, little Torah,
Let me hold you tight.
Teach me, teach me,
All the Mitzvos,
So I can do what's right.

The Torah teaches every Jew,
Torah, Torah, I love you.

תּוֹרָה צִוָּה לָנוּ מֹשֶׁה,
מוֹרָשָׁה קְהִלַּת יַעֲקֹב.

Toroh tzivo lonu Moshe
morosho kehilas Yaakov.

The Torah that Moshe commanded us is the heritage of the congregation of Yaakov.

Tzedaka, Tzedaka, Tzedaka
That is what we give,

To poor people
To help them live.

So they'll have
food and clothes,

So they'll have
food and clothes,

Even a penny a day
Before we start to pray.

Boys in the Army of Hashem
stand up:
One, two, three
One, two, three.
We are soldiers
One, two, three.

This is our uniform
as you can see,
We wear our Tzitzis and
our Yarmulke too.
'Cause that's what the Torah
tells us to do.

**בָּרוּךְ אַתָּה יְיָ, אֱלֹהֵינוּ מֶלֶךְ הָעוֹלָם, אֲשֶׁר
קִדְּשָׁנוּ בְּמִצְוֹתָיו, וְצִוָּנוּ עַל מִצְוַת צִיצִת.**

***Boruch atoh Adonoy, Eloheinu Melech ho-olom,
asher kid'shonu b'Mitzvosov, v'tzivonu al Mitzvas Tzitzis.***

*Blessed are You, Lord our G-d, King of the universe, who has sanctified us with
His commandments, and commanded us concerning the Mitzvah of Tzitzis.*

Girls in the
Army of Hashem stand up:
One, two, three
One, two, three.
We are soldiers
One, two, three.

We wear our dresses
As you can see.

We make Challah and
Light Shabbos candles too,

'Cause that's what
the Torah tells us to do.

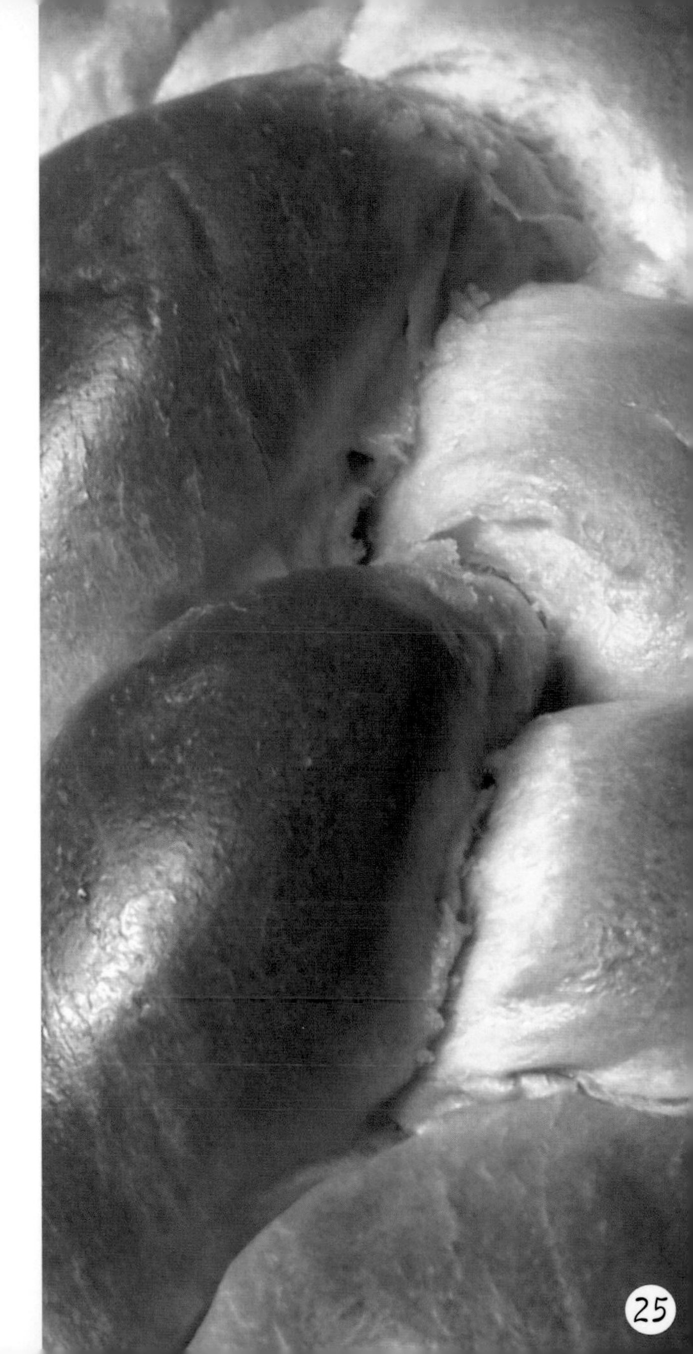

Don’t walk in front of me,
I may not follow.

Don’t walk behind me,
I may not lead.

Just walk beside me,
And be my friend.

And together we will walk,
In the way of Hashem.

וְאָהַבְתָּ לְרֵעֲךָ כָּמוֹךָ,
זֶה כְּלָל גָּדוֹל בַּתּוֹרָה (x2)

V’ohavto l’ray-acho komocho
zeh klol godol ba-Torah. (x2)

Oh let's be friends and join together,
Oh let's be friends, now and forever,
Oh let's be friends and join together,
Oh let's be friends 'cause that's the Torah way!

הֲרֵינִי מְקַבֵּל עָלַי מִצְוַת עֲשֵׂה
שֶׁל וְאָהַבְתָּ לְרֵעֲךָ כָּמוֹךָ.

Ha-rayni m'kabel olai Mitzvas asay
shel v'ohavto l'ray-acho komocho.

I hereby take upon myself to fulfill the mitzvah, "Love your fellowman as yourself."

מַה טֹּבוּ אֹהָלֶיךָ יַעֲקֹב, מִשְׁכְּנֹתֶיךָ יִשְׂרָאֵל.
וַאֲנִי בְּרֹב חַסְדְּךָ אָבֹא בֵיתֶךָ, אֶשְׁתַּחֲוֶה
אֶל הֵיכַל קָדְשְׁךָ בְּיִרְאָתֶךָ. וַאֲנִי תְפִלָּתִי
לְךָ יְיָ עֵת רָצוֹן, אֱלֹהִים בְּרָב חַסְדֶּךָ,
עֲנֵנִי בֶּאֱמֶת יִשְׁעֶךָ.

Ma tovu oholecho Yaakov, mishk'nosecho Yisroel.
Va-ani b'rov chas'd'cho ovo veisecho, eshtachaveh el heichal
kodshecho b'yirosecho. Va-ani sefilosi lecho Adonoy eis rotzon
Elohim b'rov chas'decho aneini be-emes yishecho.

How goodly are your tents, O Jacob; your dwelling places, O Israel!
And I, through Your abundant kindness, come into Your House; I bow toward Your holy sanctuary in awe of You. May my prayer to You, Lord, be at a favorable time; G-d, in Your abounding kindness, answer me with Your true deliverance.

אֲדוֹן עוֹלָם

אֲשֶׁר מָלַךְ, בְּטֶרֶם כָּל יְצוּר נִבְרָא.
לְעֵת נַעֲשָׂה בְחֶפְצוֹ כֹּל, אֲזַי מֶלֶךְ שְׁמוֹ נִקְרָא.
וְאַחֲרֵי כִּכְלוֹת הַכֹּל, לְבַדּוֹ יִמְלוֹךְ נוֹרָא. וְהוּא
הָיָה, וְהוּא הֹוֶה, וְהוּא יִהְיֶה בְּתִפְאָרָה. וְהוּא
אֶחָד וְאֵין שֵׁנִי, לְהַמְשִׁיל לוֹ לְהַחְבִּירָה. בְּלִי
רֵאשִׁית בְּלִי תַכְלִית, וְלוֹ הָעֹז וְהַמִּשְׂרָה. וְהוּא
אֵלִי וְחַי גֹּאֲלִי, וְצוּר חֶבְלִי בְּעֵת צָרָה. וְהוּא
נִסִּי וּמָנוֹס לִי, מְנָת כּוֹסִי בְּיוֹם אֶקְרָא. בְּיָדוֹ
אַפְקִיד רוּחִי, בְּעֵת אִישַׁן וְאָעִירָה. וְעִם רוּחִי
גְּוִיָּתִי, יְיָ לִי וְלֹא אִירָא.

adon olom asher molach, b'terem kol y'tzur nivro. L'eis na-aso v'cheftzo kol, azai Melech sh'mo nikro. V'a-cha-ray kichlos ha-kol l'vado yimloch noro. V'hu hoyo, V'hu hove, V'hu yih-ye b'siforo. V'hu echod v'ein sheini l'hamshil lo l'hachbiro. B'li reishis b'li sachlis v'lo ho-oz v'ha-misro. V'hu eili v'chai go-ali, v'tzur chevli b'eis tzoro. V'hu nisi umonos li, m'nos kosi b'yom ekro. B'yodo afkid ruchi, b'eis ishan v'o-iro. V'im ruchi g'vi-yosi, Adonoy li v'lo iro.

Lord of the universe, who reigned before anything was created — at the time when by His will all things were made, then was His name proclaimed King. And after all things shall cease to be, the Awesome One will reign alone. He was, He is, and He shall be in glory. He is one, and there is no other to compare to Him, to consort with Him. Without beginning, without end, power and dominion belong to Him. He is my G-d and my ever-living Redeemer, the strength of my lot in time of distress. He is my banner and my refuge, my portion on the day I call. Into His hand I entrust my spirit, when I sleep and when I wake. And with my soul, my body too, the Lord is with me, I shall not fear.

צָרְכֵי עַמְּךָ יִשְׂרָאֵל מְרוּבִּים וְדַעְתָּם קְצָרָה,
יְהִי רָצוֹן מִלְּפָנֶיךָ יְיָ אֱלֹהֵינוּ, שֶׁתִּתֵּן לְכָל
אֶחָד וְאֶחָד כְּדֵי פַּרְנָסָתוֹ, וּלְכָל גְּוִיָּה וּגְוִיָּה
דֵּי מַחְסוֹרָהּ, וְהַטּוֹב בְּעֵינֶיךָ עֲשֵׂה. בָּרוּךְ
אַתָּה יְיָ שׁוֹמֵעַ תְּפִלָּה.

Tzorchei am'cho Yisroel m'rubim v'daatom ktzoro. Y'hi rotzon mil-fonecho Adonoy, Eloheinu, she-titein l'chol echod v'echod k'dei par-no-soso, U-l'chol g'viyo u-g'viyo dei mach-soro, v'hatov b'ei-necho asei. Boruch ato Adonoy shomei-a teffiloh.

The needs of Your nation Israel are many and they don't know how to request all their needs. May it be Your will, G-d our G-d that You give each and everyone adequate sustenance, and fill everybody's want, and do that which You deem proper. Blessed are You G-d who accepts prayer.

Twinkle, Twinkle, Kochavim,
Shining in the Shomayim.

When you say Shema today,
Everything will be ok,

When you say Shema tonight,
everything will be alright.

Sh'ma Yisroel Adonoy Eloheinu, Adonoy echod.

Whisper: Boruch sheim k'vod mal'chuso l'olom vo-ed.

V'ohavto eis Adonoy Elohecho, b'chol l'vov'cho, u-v'chol naf-sh'cho, u-v'chol m'odecho. V'hoyu ha-d'vorim ho-ei-le asher onochi m'tzav'cho ha-yom al l'vovecho. V'shinantom l'vonecho v'dibarto bom, b'shiv-t'cho b'veisecho, u-v'lech-t'cho vaderech, u-v'shoch-b'cho, u-v'kumecho. U-k'shartom l'os al yodecho v'hoyu l'totofos bein einecho. U-ch'savtom al mezuzos bei-secho u-vish-orecho.

Hear, O Israel, the Lord is our G-d, the Lord is One.

Whisper: Blessed be the name of the glory of His kingdom forever and ever.

You shall love the L-rd your G-d with all your heart, with all your soul and with all your might. And these words which I command you today shall be on your heart. You shall teach them thoroughly to your children, and you shall speak of them when you sit in your house and when you walk on the road, when you lie down and when you rise up. You shall bind them as a sign upon your arm, and they shall be for a reminder between your eyes. And you shall write them upon the doorposts of your house and upon your gates.

שְׁמַע ׀ יִשְׂרָאֵל, יְיָ ׀ אֱלֹהֵינוּ, יְיָ ׀ אֶחָד.

בָּרוּךְ שֵׁם כְּבוֹד מַלְכוּתוֹ לְעוֹלָם וָעֶד.

וְאָהַבְתָּ אֵת יְיָ אֱלֹהֶיךָ, בְּכָל ׀ לְבָבְךָ, וּבְכָל נַפְשְׁךָ, וּבְכָל מְאֹדֶךָ. וְהָיוּ הַדְּבָרִים הָאֵלֶּה אֲשֶׁר אָנֹכִי מְצַוְּךָ הַיּוֹם, עַל ׀ לְבָבֶךָ. וְשִׁנַּנְתָּם לְבָנֶיךָ וְדִבַּרְתָּ בָּם, בְּשִׁבְתְּךָ בְּבֵיתֶךָ, וּבְלֶכְתְּךָ בַדֶּרֶךְ, וּבְשָׁכְבְּךָ, וּבְקוּמֶךָ. וּקְשַׁרְתָּם לְאוֹת עַל יָדֶךָ, וְהָיוּ לְטֹטָפֹת בֵּין עֵינֶיךָ. וּכְתַבְתָּם עַל מְזֻזוֹת בֵּיתֶךָ, וּבִשְׁעָרֶיךָ.

This prayer reminds us to eagerly pray for Moshiach. It is our strongest wish that Moshiach should come and rebuild the Beis Hamikdosh in Jerusalem.

שֶׁיִּבָּנֶה בֵּית הַמִּקְדָּשׁ בִּמְהֵרָה בְיָמֵינוּ, וְתֵן חֶלְקֵנוּ בְּתוֹרָתֶךָ.

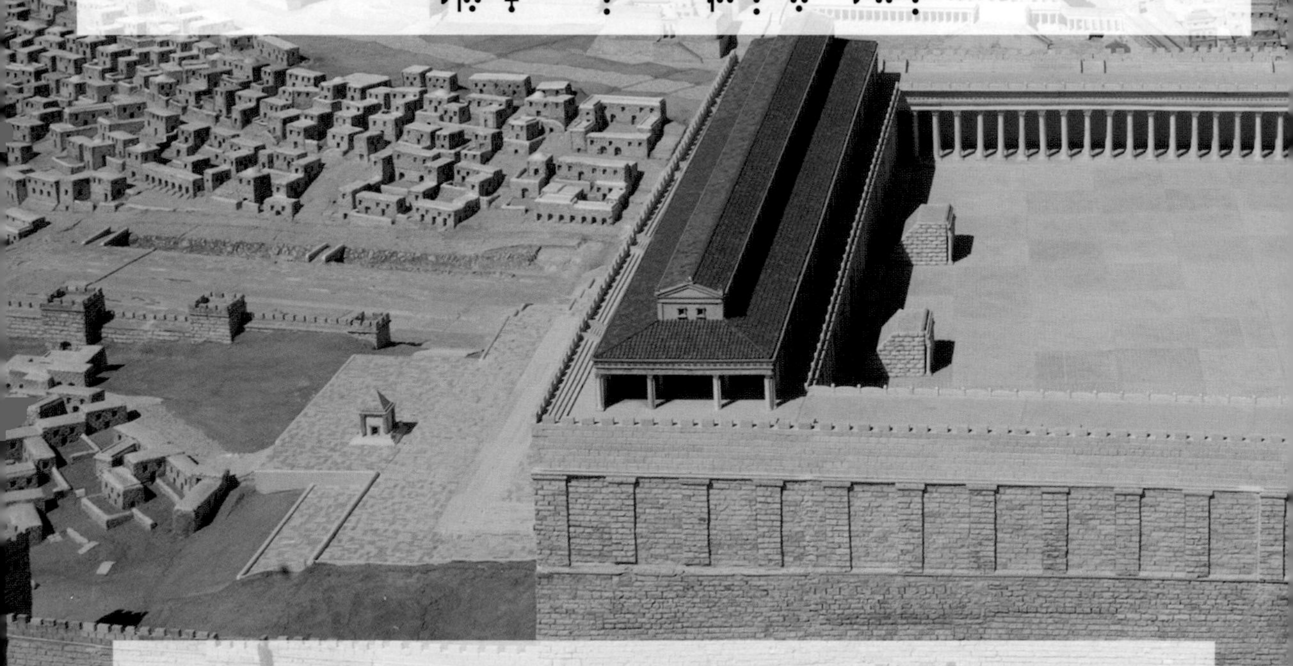

She-yibone Beis Hamikdosh bim'heiro v'yomeinu
v'sein chelkeinu b'sorosecho. *(x2)*

Please build us the Beis Hamikdosh,
build us the Beis Hamikdosh,
we really, really, really, want it now, right now! *(x2)*

This verse reminds us that righteous people are especially dear to Hashem, and they will merit the world to come.

אַךְ צַדִּיקִים יוֹדוּ לִשְׁמֶךָ,
יֵשְׁבוּ יְשָׁרִים אֶת פָּנֶיךָ.

Ach tzadikim yodu lishmecho yeishvu y'shorim es ponecho.

Way up high, in the sky
There's a building still not finished.
Way up high, in the sky
There's a Mikdash Hashlishi.

And for every Mitzvah,
that we do so carefully,
Hashem adds a brick,
to the Mikdash Hashlishi.

אֲנִי מַאֲמִין בֶּאֱמוּנָה שְׁלֵמָה
בְּבִיאַת הַמָּשִׁיחַ אֲנִי מַאֲמִין.

Ani maamin b'emuna sh'leimo
b'vias ha-Moshiach ani maamin (x2)
We want Moshiach,
We want Moshiach Now (x3)
We want Moshiach, Moshiach Now!

Omar Rabbi Akivo, omar Rabbi Akivo,
v'ohavto l'ray-acho komocho. **(x2)**
Sheli, sheloch, sheloch, sheloch. **(x2)**
Zeh klol godol ba-Torah.

אָמַר רַבִּי עֲקִיבָא, אָמַר רַבִּי עֲקִיבָא,
וְאָהַבְתָּ לְרֵעֲךָ כָּמוֹךָ, (x2)
שֶׁלִּי, שֶׁלָּךְ, שֶׁלָּךְ, שֶׁלָּךְ, (x2)
זֶה כְּלָל גָּדוֹל בַּתּוֹרָה.

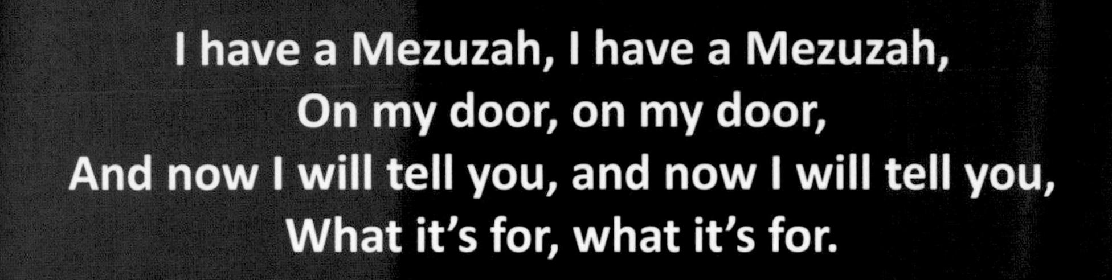

I have a Mezuzah, I have a Mezuzah,
On my door, on my door,
And now I will tell you, and now I will tell you,
What it's for, what it's for.

To kiss the Mezuzah, to kiss the Mezuzah,
Is our aim, is our aim
For on it is written, for on it is written
Hashem's name, Hashem's name.

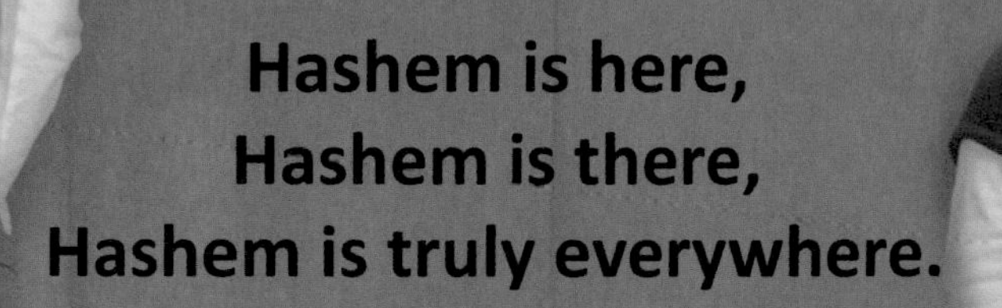

Hashem is here,
Hashem is there,
Hashem is truly everywhere.

Hashem is here,
Hashem is there,
Hashem is truly everywhere.

Up up,
Down down,
Right left,
And all around,
Here there,
And everywhere,
That's where
He can be found. (x2)

12 TORAH Passages:

תּוֹרָה צִוָּה לָנוּ מֹשֶׁה
מוֹרָשָׁה קְהִלַּת יַעֲקֹב.

Toroh tzivo lonu Moshe morosho kehilas Yaakov.

"The Torah that Moshe commanded us is the heritage of the congregation of Yaakov." ***(Deut. 33:4)***

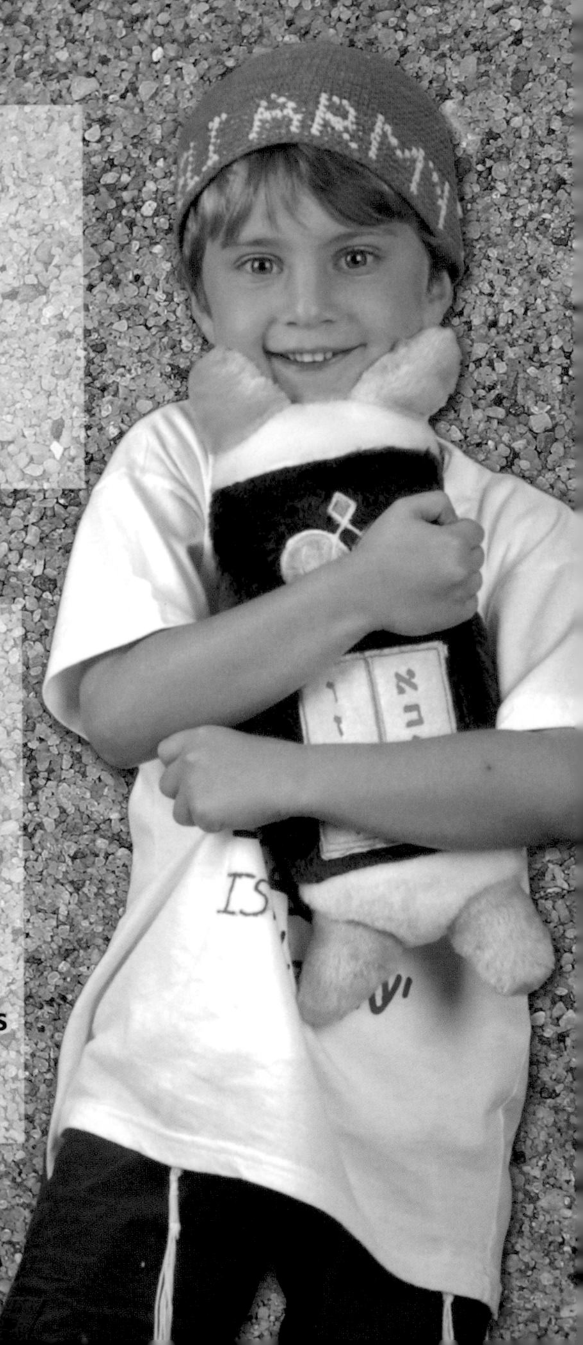

שְׁמַע יִשְׂרָאֵל ה׳ אֱלֹהֵינוּ ה׳ אֶחָד.

Sh'ma Yisroel Adonoy Eloheinu, Adonoy echod.

"Hear O Israel, the Lord is our G-d, the Lord is One." ***(Deut. 6:4)***

בְּכָל דּוֹר וָדוֹר חַיָּב אָדָם לִרְאוֹת אֶת עַצְמוֹ כְּאִלּוּ הוּא יָצָא מִמִּצְרָיִם.

B'chol dor vo-dor chayov odom li-ros es atzmo k'ilu hu yotzo mi-Mitzrayim.

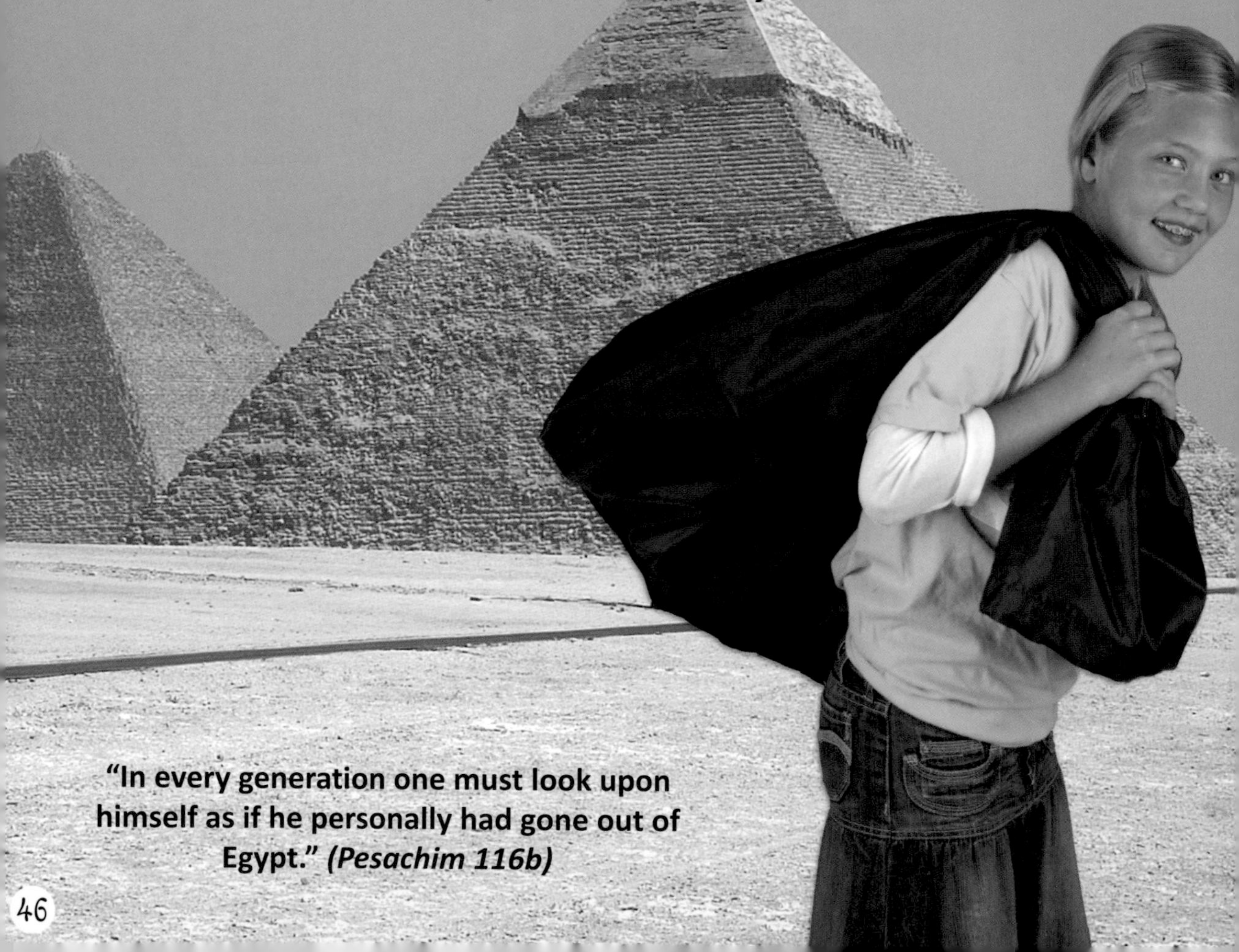

"In every generation one must look upon himself as if he personally had gone out of Egypt." ***(Pesachim 116b)***

כָּל יִשְׂרָאֵל יֵשׁ לָהֶם חֵלֶק לְעוֹלָם הַבָּא שֶׁנֶּאֱמַר וְעַמֵּךְ כּוּלָם צַדִּיקִים לְעוֹלָם יִירְשׁוּ אָרֶץ נֵצֶר מַטָּעַי מַעֲשֵׂה יָדַי לְהִתְפָּאֵר.

Kol Yisroel yesh lo-hem cheleck l'olom habo, she-ne-emar v'amech kulom tzadikim l'olom yirshu oretz netzer ma-toai ma-asei yodai l'hispoer.

"All Israel have a share in the World To Come, as it is stated *(Isaiah 60:21)*: 'And Your people are all *tzadikim* (righteous). They shall inherit the land forever. They are the branch of My planting, the work of My hands, in which I take pride.'" *(Sanhedrin 90a)*

Ki korov eilecho hadovor m'od, b'ficho, u-vil-vov'cho la-a-soso.

"It is within your close reach to follow the Torah in speech, feeling and deed." ***(Deut. 30:14)***
(As explained in the Tanya)

וְהִנֵּה ה׳ נִצָּב עָלָיו וּמְלֹא כָל הָאָרֶץ כְּבוֹדוֹ וּמַבִּיט עָלָיו וּבוֹחֵן כְּלָיוֹת וָלֵב אִם עוֹבְדוֹ כָּרָאוּי.

V'hinei Hashem nitzov olov u-m'lo chol ho-oretz k'vodo umabit olov uvochein k'loyos voleiv im ovdo ko-ro-uy.

"G-d stands over him, and the whole earth is full of His glory, and He searches his mind and heart (to see) if he is serving Him as is fitting."
(Tanya, chap. 41)

בְּרֵאשִׁית בָּרָא אֱלֹהִים אֵת הַשָּׁמַיִם וְאֵת הָאָרֶץ.

B'reishis boro Elohim eis ha-shomayim v'eis ho-oretz.

"In the beginning G-d created the heavens and the earth." *(Genesis 1:1)*

וְשִׁנַּנְתָּם לְבָנֶיךָ וְדִבַּרְתָּ בָּם בְּשִׁבְתְּךָ בְּבֵיתֶךָ וּבְלֶכְתְּךָ בַדֶּרֶךְ וּבְשָׁכְבְּךָ וּבְקוּמֶךָ.

V'shinantom l'vonecho v'dibarto bom, b'shiv-t'cho b'veisecho, u-v'lech-t'cho vaderech, u-v'shoch-b'cho, u-v'kumecho.

"And you shall teach the Torah to your children, and you should speak about it when you are home and when you travel, before you lie down to sleep and when you wake up." ***(Deut. 6:7)***

יָגַעְתִּי וְלֹא מָצָאתִי אַל תַּאֲמִין: לֹא יָגַעְתִּי וּמָצָאתִי אַל תַּאֲמִין: יָגַעְתִּי וּמָצָאתִי תַּאֲמִין.

Yo-gati v'lo motzosi, al taamin. Lo yo-gati umotzosi, al taamin. Yo-gati umotzosi, taamin.

If someone says, "I have worked hard, and I have not been successful," don't believe him. If someone says, "I have not worked hard and I have been successful," don't believe him. If someone says, "I have worked hard and I have been successful," believe him!!! *(Megilla, 6b)*

וְאָהַבְתָּ לְרֵעֲךָ כָּמוֹךָ
רַבִּי עֲקִיבָא אוֹמֵר זֶה כְּלָל גָּדוֹל בַּתּוֹרָה.

V'ohavto l'ray-acho komocho, Rabbi Akivo omer, zeh klol godol ba-Toroh.

Rabbi Akiva says that, "To love your fellow as yourself, is a great basic principle of the Torah." ***(Levit. 19:18, Midrash)***

וְזֶה כָּל הָאָדָם וְתַכְלִית בְּרִיאָתוֹ וּבְרִיאַת כָּל הָעוֹלָמוֹת עֶלְיוֹנִים וְתַחְתּוֹנִים לִהְיוֹת לוֹ דִירָה זוֹ בְּתַחְתּוֹנִים.

V'zeh kol ho-odom v'sachlis bri-oso u-vrias kol ho-olomos elyonim v'tachtonim, lihiyos lo diro zo b'tachtonim.

"The purpose of the creation of every Jew and of all the worlds is to make a dwelling place for G-d in this world." ***(Tanya, Chap. 33)***

יִשְׂמַח יִשְׂרָאֵל בְּעוֹשָׂיו פֵּירוּשׁ
שֶׁכָּל מִי שֶׁהוּא מִזֶּרַע יִשְׂרָאֵל יֵשׁ לוֹ לִשְׂמוֹחַ
בְּשִׂמְחַת ה' אֲשֶׁר שָׂשׂ וְשָׂמֵחַ בְּדִירָתוֹ בְּתַחְתּוֹנִים.

Yismach Yisroel b'osov; peirush, shekol mi she-hu mizera Yisroel yesh lo lismoach b'simchas Hashem, asher sos v'someach b'diroso b'tachtonim.

"The Jews should rejoice in their Maker. Every Jew should share in G-d's joy, Who rejoices and is happy in His dwelling place in this world." *(Tanya, Chap. 33)*

Kiddush

On drinking wine or grape juice:

בָּרוּךְ אַתָּה יְיָ,
אֱלֹהֵינוּ מֶלֶךְ הָעוֹלָם,
בּוֹרֵא פְּרִי הַגָּפֶן.

Boruch ato Adonoy,
Eloheinu Melech
ho-olom, borei
p'ri ha-gofen.

Blessed are You,
Lord our G-d,
King of the universe,
who creates
the fruit of the vine.

Blessings

The blessing to say before eating bread:

בָּרוּךְ אַתָּה יְיָ, אֱלֹהֵינוּ מֶלֶךְ הָעוֹלָם,
הַמּוֹצִיא לֶחֶם מִן הָאָרֶץ.

Boruch ato Adonoy, Eloheinu Melech ho-olom,
ha-motzi lechem min ho-oretz.

Blessed are You, Lord our G-d, King of the universe,
who brings forth bread from the earth.

Before eating cake, cookies, cereals or any food containing the 5 kinds of grain: wheat, barley, spelt, oats and rye, say the following blessing:

בָּרוּךְ אַתָּה יְיָ, אֱלֹהֵינוּ מֶלֶךְ הָעוֹלָם, בּוֹרֵא מִינֵי מְזוֹנוֹת.

Boruch ato Adonoy, Eloheinu Melech ho-olom, borei minei m'zonos.

Blessed are You, Lord our G-d, King of the universe,
who creates various kinds of food.

Before eating all tree-grown fruits, except bananas, say the following blessing:

בָּרוּךְ אַתָּה יְיָ, אֱלֹהֵינוּ מֶלֶךְ הָעוֹלָם, בּוֹרֵא פְּרִי הָעֵץ.

Boruch ato Adonoy, Eloheinu Melech ho-olom, borei p'ri ho-eitz.

Blessed are You, Lord our G-d, King of the universe, who creates the fruit of the tree.

Before eating earth grown fruits and vegetables, say the following blessing:

בָּרוּךְ אַתָּה יְיָ, אֱלֹהֵינוּ מֶלֶךְ הָעוֹלָם,
בּוֹרֵא פְּרִי הָאֲדָמָה.

Boruch ato Adonoy, Eloheinu Melech ho-olom borei p'ri ho-adomo.

Blessed are You, Lord our G-d, King of the universe, who creates the fruit of the earth.

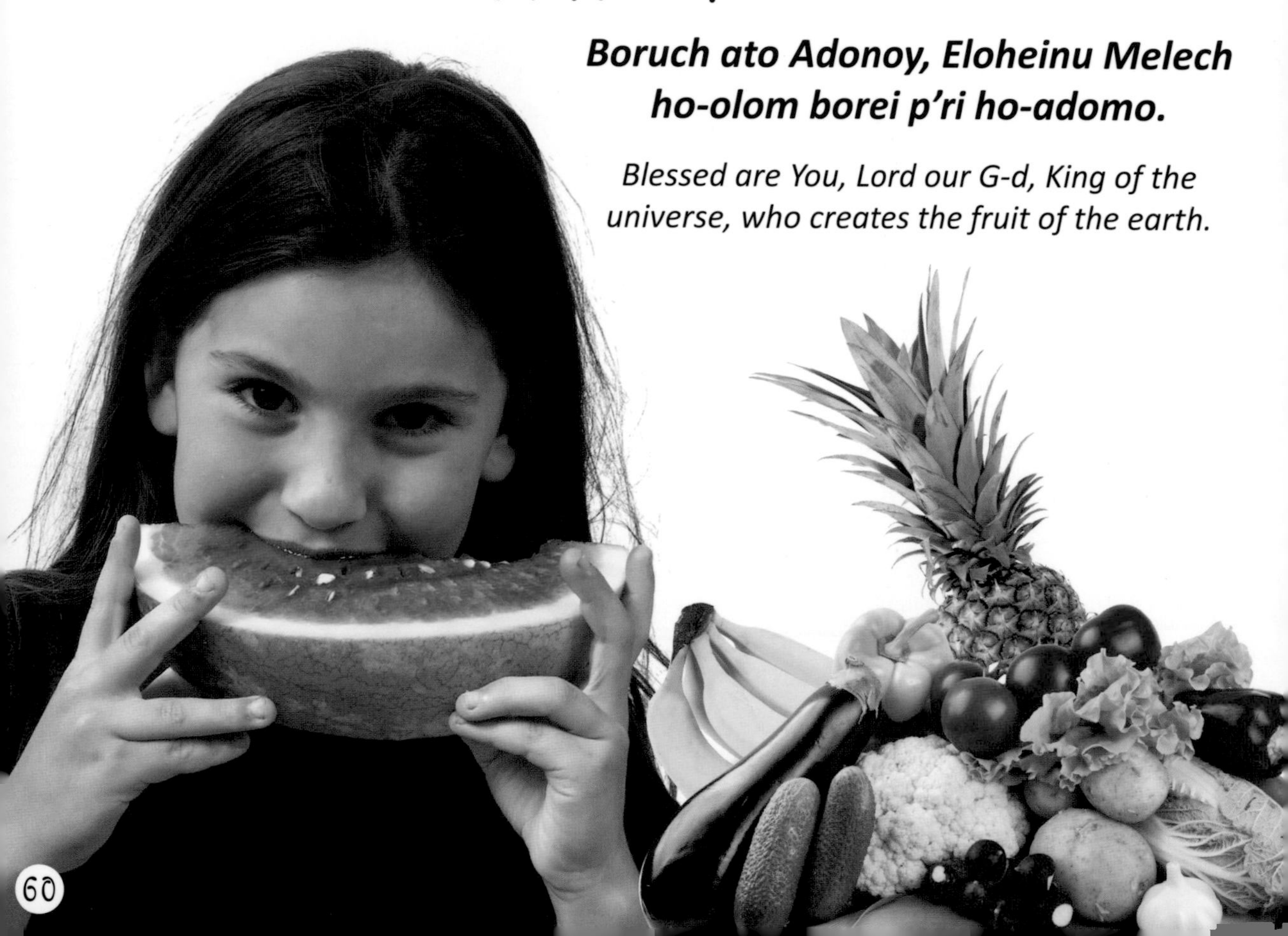

Before eating all foods <u>not</u> grown in the earth or on trees, like meat, fish, milk, eggs, cheese, candy, mushrooms and liquids (except wine), say the following blessing:

בָּרוּךְ אַתָּה יְיָ, אֱלֹהֵינוּ מֶלֶךְ הָעוֹלָם, שֶׁהַכֹּל נִהְיָה בִּדְבָרוֹ.

Boruch ato Adonoy, Eloheinu Melech ho-olom, she-hakol nihiyo bi-d'voro.

Blessed are You, Lord our G-d, King of the universe, by whose word all things came to be.

Grace After Meals

After a meal with bread say:

בְּרִיךְ רַחֲמָנָא, אֱלָהָנָא, מַלְכָּא דְעָלְמָא, מָרָא דְהַאי פִּיתָא.

Brich rach-a-mono Elohono, malko d'olmo moro d'hai pito.

Blessed is Hashem our G–d,
King of the universe,
Master of this bread.

When hearing thunder we say:

בָּרוּךְ אַתָּה יְיָ, אֱלֹהֵינוּ מֶלֶךְ הָעוֹלָם,
שֶׁכֹּחוֹ וּגְבוּרָתוֹ מָלֵא עוֹלָם.

Boruch ato Adonoy, Eloheinu Melech ho-olom, shekocho u-g'vuroso molei olom.

Blessed are You, Lord our G-d, King of the universe, whose strength and might fills the world.

Upon seeing lightning we say:

בָּרוּךְ אַתָּה יְיָ,
אֱלֹהֵינוּ מֶלֶךְ הָעוֹלָם,
עוֹשֶׂה מַעֲשֵׂה בְרֵאשִׁית.

Boruch ato Adonoy, Eloheinu Melech ho-olom, osei ma-asei b'reishis

Blessed are You, Lord our G-d, King of the universe, who makes the work of creation.

When seeing a rainbow we say:

בָּרוּךְ אַתָּה יְיָ, אֱלֹהֵינוּ מֶלֶךְ הָעוֹלָם, זוֹכֵר הַבְּרִית, וְנֶאֱמָן בִּבְרִיתוֹ, וְקַיָּם בְּמַאֲמָרוֹ.

Boruch ato Adonoy, Eloheinu Melech ho-olom, zocher ha-bris v'ne-emon bivriso, v'kayom b'ma-a-moro.

Blessed are You, Lord our G-d, King of the universe, who remembers the covenant and is faithful to G-d's covenant and keeps G-d's promise.

Shabbos Candles

With your eyes covered, recite the blessing:

בָּרוּךְ אַתָּה יְיָ, אֱלֹהֵינוּ מֶלֶךְ הָעוֹלָם,
אֲשֶׁר קִדְּשָׁנוּ בְּמִצְוֹתָיו,
וְצִוָּנוּ לְהַדְלִיק נֵר
שֶׁל שַׁבָּת קֹדֶשׁ.

Boruch ato Adonoy, Eloheinu Melech ho-olom, asher kid'shonu b'Mitzvosov, v'tzivonu l'hadlik ner shel Shabbos kodesh.

Blessed are You, Lord our G-d, King of the universe, who has sanctified us with His commandments, and commanded us to kindle the light of the holy Shabbos.

Glossary

12 Torah Passages - *Verses and sayings of our sages, which the Lubavitcher Rebbe taught for every child to learn and recite each day*

Aleph Beis - *Hebrew Alphabet*

B'nei Yisroel - *Jewish People*

Beis Hamikdosh - *Holy Temple*

Challah - *Challah the bread loaves customarily eaten at the Shabbos meals*

Hashem - *G-d*

Kiddush - *Blessing recited over wine on the Shabbos eve and day and on Jewish Holidays*

Mezuzah - *Handwritten parchment scroll with the text of the 'Shema' and affixed to the doorposts of Jewish homes and buildings*

Mikdash Hashlishi - *The 3rd Holy Temple*

Mitzvah - *One of the 613 commandments; a good deed*

Mitzvos - *Commandments of the Torah*

Modeh Ani - *Morning prayer of thanks said upon awakening*

Moshiach - *Redeemer (Messiah)*

Na-aseh V'nishma - *"We will do and we will hear/understand." The response of the Jewish people to observe the laws of the Torah, and only afterward to study these laws to understand them*

Neshama - *Soul*

Shabbos - *Sabbath*

Shema - *The "Hear O Israel" prayer declaring that Hashem is One.*

Shomayim - *Heaven*

Siddur - *Prayer book*

Torah - *The Five Books of Moses; Jewish Scripture and Oral Tradition*

Tzedaka - *Charity*

Tzitzis - *A four cornered garment with strings attached worn by Jewish boys. The Torah commands us to wear tzitzis (fringes) at the corners of our garments as a reminder of the mitzvos.*

Yadayim - *Hands*

Yarmulke - *Skull Cap*

The My First Sing-Along Siddur
is dedicated to the loving memory
of two very good friends
Arturo Colodner - Shmuel ben Tzvi OBM
and
Mauricio Fuchs - Mordechai ben Avraham OBM

Arturo & Mauricio
loved to come
to The Shul each week
to Daven with their children.

Through this siddur they will continue
to be with their children
as they daven
each and every day.

Memorex
REPEAT
PROG
MASTER VOLUME
MIC VOLUME